DIETS ARE STUPID! JUST READ THIS INSTEAD

How to use your ridiculously clever mind to lose weight easily. No starving, stupid diets, or suffering needed.

Declan Carroll

Will you do me a favour?

When you list books on Amazon, reviews are a big help to get your book noticed. If you would be kind enough to take time out of your busy day to provide a review, I am pretty sure good things will happen in your future! Just go to Amazon and follow the **"Write a customer review"** link.

Thanks for your support!

Table of Contents

Introduction

Welcome to a book that is as much about the change in mindset required to be the type of person that actually finishes and publishes a book (you know, as opposed to just saying it!), as it is a weight loss guide. What? Have you been tricked into reading some hippie, mindfulness nonsense rather than an actual weight loss book...not quite, but sort of!

While I am not going to give you the hippie nonsense, I will be showing you what worked for me, and it is as much about the different person you need to become, as it is the food you eat and strategies you employ to accelerate the weight loss. Don't worry, there will be strategies to follow too, but that part is easy! I am working on the premise that people are not stupid and already know the good food from the bad.

The big challenge, as you will soon learn, is that I believe we have all been tricked into how we perceive food, and now think we want the rubbish food that is causing us to become overweight, sick, and on track for type 2 diabetes, and an early grave. When this perception is combined with a mind that has resigned itself to staying big, it is no wonder so many of us are struggling!

The good news is that once you read this book and if I've explained myself well enough, you will be able to free yourself from the mental torture of trying to "be good" and avoiding foods that you really want to eat. You will be in a state of calmness and feel like you are getting away with something, being able to easily pass on the rubbish food and eat as much as you wish of the good stuff that humans were designed to eat. Ready? Let's go!

So Why Should You Listen to Me? What Do I Know?

Excellent question. Why should you listen to some guy writing a book? I am not a doctor, dietitian, nutritionist, fitness instructor, scientist, journalist, nor do I belong to any other profession that might claim to be an expert in the field of humans losing weight. I haven't completed my own studies nor have I taken a bunch of big people and made them eat nothing but salads and run all day while a drill sergeant type of 'trainer' screams at them to "keep going maggot, twenty more press-ups, you wussy piece of s@&t!"

So…..why then? Well, I believe I have figured out this weight loss puzzle and I want to share it with you. But guess what, when I say I have figured it out, I have figured out what works for <u>me,</u> and want to invite you to consider this book as a guide to see if you can get the same results. I am not guaranteeing anything. I am not you, nor can I get into your head and see things the same way you do. Your body is not the same as mine nor the next person's. It is all theory until you actually try it out yourself.

I'm also not claiming that you should blindly follow what I say. An excellent quote from the great Jim Rohn (Jim's the guy that mentored Tony Robbins, who more people tend to have heard of) is "be a student, not a follower". You are responsible for you, so do your due diligence and think for yourself. Take what is helpful from this book and consider the points that I make, but definitely use your own noggin when it comes to deciding what is good for you. You might completely disagree with some of what I say, and that is fine. All I ask is you see this short book through and have an open mind!

Disclaimer. I was not a morbidly obese person. This is not a story of someone that was on the brink of death and lost 70 percent of their body weight to save their life. I have, however, been someone with a bit of Irritable Bowel Syndrome (IBS), which led me to experiment with my diet over the years. I also simply wanted to go from a bit of a dad body, but reasonably fit and healthy, to really fit and really healthy, including getting my weight to a level that I was happy would allow me to live a longer life. I had a new baby on the way, which gave me an extra "why". That always helps. Being pulled is much easier than pushing yourself.

When I started this book, I intended to create any easy-to-read and practical guide to help those that are determined to lose some weight and make a change in their health. This book is deliberately a short read, which will hopefully ensure that even those reluctant readers can get through it and take advantage of the content.

Do You Actually Need to Lose Weight?

Only you can answer that one. There was once a time where the younger and more stupid version of me would judge people based on their weight. I would see someone who I perceived as overweight, and I would observe them at the supermarket, plodding along, filling their trolley with cola, bread, chips, and other rubbish, and think to myself "what are they doing to themselves? They must know that they look that way, why don't they do something about it?". What a dumbass I was. Of course, they knew how they looked. With people like me staring and judging them all the time, how could they forget? Who the hell was I to judge someone else in this way?

People are allowed to live their lives however they please. The older and, hopefully, wiser me knows that I should be concentrating on myself first and not worry about some stranger at the supermarket, who I know nothing about! Maybe that person is completely content and happy in life and while they likely have health issues and a shorter lifespan than others, that is their choice. Maybe there is an underlying health issue that is causing them to retain weight. Maybe they have struggled with their weight all of their life and have genuinely wanted to lose weight, but just haven't managed to find what works for them. Or maybe, and most importantly, it is none of my damn business!!

This means that if you are reading this and think the ideas I share do not suit you, that is fine with me. If your body is leaning towards the larger side and you're unhappy with your weight, I would love for this book to be a revelation and a way for you to finally lose that weight and never have to look back. However, if you decide this is not for you, I would encourage you to do two things:

1-   Share this book with a friend, who may find it valuable (sharing is caring).

2-   Make peace with yourself. If you decide that you are not prepared to make the changes required to lose weight, don't make excuses or blame others, just own it. Being at peace with your decision gives you the power to move on, with a view of yourself that is grounded in reality (I suspect if you are sensible enough to take this mature position, you will likely want to try what this book suggests anyway).

On the other hand, if you wake up in the morning and don't like the look of your waistline or can't seem to fit into the clothes you once wore, this might be for you. If you feel like you have tried everything and still can't lose weight, this might be for you. If you grew up in the 80s and 90s like me, there were terrible guidelines and advice for 'healthy' eating that persist to this day. This book is designed to help you change some of the habits that you have adopted after such terrible public dietary advice.

DIETS ARE STUPID!

Part 1- Use Your Mind to Become a Thin and Healthy Person

I am certain that transforming your body is more about unravelling a mental tangle than the actual diet you choose, so I am going to borrow a concept from a great book that played a huge part in my life, particularly, my ability to change aspects of my life that I was unhappy with. In *"The Easy Way to Quit Smoking"* by Allen Carr, Allen has the reader continue to smoke while reading the book, so as not to feel deprived or lack concentration while taking in the all-important material. Allen's view was that if you take away smoking before understanding the underlying issues causing you to light up a cigarette in the first place, you are already on the back foot and likely to fail. It is much more important to be able to take in the material in a calm and peaceful state.

If it helps you, then feel free to do the same thing while reading this book. No, I don't mean start smoking! I mean if you are not ready to change to a healthier way of eating just yet, then don't worry too much about it until you have finished the book. What is more important is that you take in the material with a calm and open mind.

That's right. You are a grown-up, eat whatever you please while reading this book. The reason I say this, is similar to Mr. Carr's theory on smoking: it is much more important that the required changes in your mind are understood, as once it all becomes clear and the nonsense and mistruths are debunked, the actual process of losing the weight will be enjoyable and can be started with feelings of confidence and empowerment, rather than fear, deprivation, and that lingering doubt that traditional dieting brings. You know, the one at the back of your mind that says, "there is no way this will last". You know the one, right? I sure do!

Wait, doesn't Allen Carr do a weight loss book? He sure does. I have read it, but found that it didn't resonate with me. Try it for yourself if you like. There are a number of weight loss books and I am sure some of them could work for you. I am really not the type to blindly claim that I know everything, let alone claim that only this book could ever work for you. However, in saying this, I am confident that this book has everything you need.

For Things to Change for You, You Need to Change

I've already quoted Jim Rohn in this book! He must have known a thing or two, because here are a few more nuggets from Jim: *"For things to change for you, you have to change"*, and *"It's not what you get, it's what you become that matters"*. Think about both of these statements for a moment.

Have you ever told yourself, "That's it, no more junk food for me"? Maybe you even managed to say "No!" to yourself for a period of time while navigating through social occasions, shared meal days at the office, and other situations that place you in the precarious position of sugar and junk-food being available, which you have to turn down, much to the astonishment of those around you? Have you ever tried to convince yourself that you can do it, maybe even shown some fleeting determination in front of others, only to sneak in that bad food late at night when no one is looking? I definitely have!

Some people even manage to lose significant amounts of weight for a while. They get comments from their friends and family - "Sally has lost weight, good for her". Sally feels great about this, but unfortunately, slowly by surely, the weight comes back on. Sally then tries to trick herself or attempts to get back on the wagon, but eventually, all the weight is back!

Why would this be? Despite losing weight for a time and probably feeling quite chuffed with herself for a while, why has Sally gone back to her old ways? Did her diet stop working? No…. I repeat, No, the diet didn't suddenly stop working. **It is because Sally didn't change the type of person that she was!** What I mean by that is that is while the physical appearance of Sally may have changed, at least temporarily, Sally failed to address her underlying issues with food, the story she tells herself, and her deep-seated and often subconscious identity as a big person, that have sabotaged her in the past. You may be familiar with some of this self-talk:

1. I just don't have the will power needed.
2. Life is too short not to enjoy food.
3. This is going well, but it won't last.
4. What will other people think?
5. It's easy for you, blah blah blah…
6. It's my vice.
7. It's someone else's fault.

I maintain that if you can address this self-talk and debunk some of the myths and misconceptions, you will be on your way to changing who you are. You will soon become the type of person that maintains a healthy weight. Combine this with knowing what and when to eat and the skinnier version of you will be ready to see the world. So, get excited about the new you, and let's get started with the transformation in your thinking, by addressing each of these statements, as well as clearing up a few other things:

I Just Don't Have the Will Power Needed

This is garbage. Not that you do or do not have the necessary will power, but the term itself is flawed. Will power is one of the most annoying and overused terms in the English language. Think about the words for a moment. The power of your will. To me, the term is referring to your ability to keep doing something using your mind as the force or energy behind it. Have you ever seen the show Survivor? Sure you have. If you haven't, the show takes a bunch of people and places them on an island or some isolated location, and film them as they go through life in their 'tribes' — the objective is to vote each other off until only one person is left.

Anyway, I think of will power when I see the challenges that are set for the contestants as part of this show. Sometimes they are required to balance atop a thin wooden structure or hold a rope above their heads, and the last one to fall off or drop their arms, wins. This means that they have to outlast the other contestants in a challenge that may seem physical, but is really a mental battle of wills, designed to last for hours, to see which contestant is capable of not giving in until they are the last person standing. This is how I think of will power.

The problem with will power, at least to me, is that something that requires will power indicates that endurance of pain or discomfort is required. That you don't really want to do it and you need to "resist the temptation" and use your will power to say "no" to yourself. The obvious issue with this is that it would create stress and feelings of deprivation. This applies not only to eating, but to any number of things. If you are convinced that will power is the only way to lose weight, you may be able to do it for a while (maybe forever), but you won't have the sense of freedom and peace that comes with changing your thinking, and therefore, changing who are. This would not be a successful outcome. I want you to be happy and free of the 'will power' approach to food.

Forgetting about using will power as an option is really important, so let me use an example to explain this further. Let's say that Tom has a problem with drinking coffee. Let's also say that you don't. Tom drinks 15 cups per day and desperately wants to cut down to 3. Tom loves coffee and feels he cannot get through the day without it. By asking him to cut down on coffee, in his mind, you may as well ask him to cut off his hand and give it to you! By the way, I am not saying coffee is good or bad for you, I'm merely using it as an example. On the other hand, a casual coffee drinker like you, may usually have a cup in the morning and the occasional cup socially. You can take it or leave it.

Your views on coffee are clearly very different from Tom's. If you were both asked to drink no coffee for a week, how do you think each of you would feel? How would each person get through the week? I believe Tom would be terrified. If he embarked on this week, he would likely tell himself that will power is what he will require to do this. The problem would be that he is going to need extreme will power to overcome the mental turmoil that will go on while he 'suffers' from withdrawal and feelings of deprivation, while 'detoxing' from coffee.

What about you, the casual coffee drinker? Let's say there was some minor incentive offered that was important enough for you to give up your daily coffee (remember you do enjoy it, so there needs to be a reason to not have it), say a worthwhile sum of money or tickets to your favourite band. If you had the incentive, do you think will power would be required? I believe that you would simply choose not to drink the coffee and for the first few days, you might need to remind yourself not to make the coffee at your usual time. Aside from a small change of routine, you wouldn't be up at night thinking about coffee, or climbing the walls with feelings of deprivation. After not having the coffee at your usual time, you would likely not even think about it again for the rest of the day.

Why not? We both know the answer is that you simply don't feel that way about coffee. You think of coffee as something that you can take or leave. You find it pleasant to have a cup, but afterward, don't give it a second thought. You certainly don't have any underlying, maniacal urge to go and make yourself another dozen cups throughout the day, to get you through! Your mindset is completely different from that of Tom and therefore, will power is not needed by you. Instead, all that is needed is a decision to change and make a small change to your routine. I repeat, will power is not needed here!

What about Tom? Now poor Tom, getting by on will power, would be having a nightmare of a time. He would likely need to mentally prepare himself before even starting. This would involve 'talking himself into it' and possibly some sort of magnificent final binge on coffee, knowing that he is about to stop. As the date gets closer, Tom's feelings of dread would build up. He would likely have a terrible sleep the night before, with his mind thinking through all the ways he can get himself out of this situation. He would tell himself that he is not ready, or he just needs a few more days to prepare. He might think to himself that he will cut back for a while beforehand. Sounds familiar when planning your diet?

Let's say, in spite of these feelings, Tom starts the cold turkey coffee challenge. His will power is at its strongest on day one. "I can do this", Tom tells himself. For the first morning, Tom does really well. He has a small headache, but his will power is getting him through. Actually, Tom has very strong will power (many would quit before lunch, but not our Tom, he's a trooper), and he makes it through all of day one! Tom feels awful, but is happy with his effort. Day two arrives, and Tom is able to skip his morning coffee (his favourite) and goes to work thinking "if I can just get through the day". Unfortunately for Tom, his day is about to go downhill bigtime. His super helpful boss has decided that the team has been doing well and orders coffee for everyone. "What are you having Tom?". Tom has a problem here. His will power is now feeling pretty flimsy. The mental torture is too much. Every part of Tom's being wants to say yes to that coffee. His will power is no match for the feelings he has towards his precious coffee. "Get me a latte please", comes out of Tom's mouth, "with two sugars". Tom tells himself he will get back off the coffee tomorrow, but deep down, Tom knows he is defeated.

So, what went wrong for Tom? Just as we both knew that you, the casual coffee drinker, did not need will power to stop (or at least very little will power), Tom had a mental 'mess' to untangle. His feelings towards coffee are so deeply ingrained that there was no way he was ever going to succeed. The reason being, he viewed will power as his only way of succeeding. This meant that even if he did get through the week and went on to continue to resist coffee; unless Tom managed to become a non-coffee drinker (in his mind) along the way, he would never feel happy, as he would forever feel deprived. If I were a betting man, I would say it would only be a matter of time before Tom went back to coffee, and not long before being back to 15 cups per day.

I am sure some of you will say, "Wait a minute. Tom is suffering from a physical addiction to coffee. Undoing the mental aspect won't help the fact that he is physically addicted". As with so many subjects now, you can go to Google and read as much as you like about coffee addiction and physical withdrawals. I believe that the physical withdrawal when the supply of coffee is cut off is only ever going to be a minor feeling. Like most addictions, the mental torture that goes on is what causes the feelings of suffering associated with the withdrawal.

The same goes for food. They say sugar is addictive. I am sure it is, but the definition of addictive needs to be looked at. The word addictive has taken on a whole new meaning in our culture. We have started associating the word addictive, with a lack of responsibility. You know, Sally is addicted to sweets, which is why she is fat. Or in other words, Sally is addicted, and therefore, there is nothing she can do about, so it is someone else's fault. There is no way this mentality is going to help you. I cover blaming others later in the book, but remember, as soon as you start blaming external factors for your weight, you lose all the power and give away your ability to change. Don't do it, Stuart!

Does Tom's relationship with coffee sound familiar to yours with food? Do you now see that will power is not the answer? If you are still not convinced, read this section again. Give the idea some thought, mull it over, and think it through. If you were lean and healthy, do you think you would wrestle daily with thoughts of deprivation, sadness, or discontent because of having to deny yourself of the treats that you crave deep down? Of course not. Just like the casual coffee drinker doesn't have to stop themselves from drinking a silly amount of coffee, a lean and healthy person doesn't need to use will power to stop themselves from gorging on junk food. They are lean and healthy, so why would they do that? See what I am saying? No will power is needed when you are not that kind of person.

You may be thinking, "well that's great for lean and healthy people, but I can't simply stop wanting the bad food. That's why I am overweight". Au contraire, what I am asserting is that you can stop wanting that kind of food. You absolutely can change your mindset to be the kind of person that would see a table full of cakes and biscuits, sausage rolls and slices, and instead of seeing tasty treats, you will see the food for what it is....poison that will slowly kill you!

Now I get that you are unlikely to believe this just yet. If you were raised in most Western countries, you will have been subjected to a lifetime of influence from family, friends, movies, advertising, work colleagues, and countless others, that have shaped your feelings about food. There is also a lifetime of your own habits and attachment to food. These feelings are deeply ingrained and will take a bit of focus and thought to change, but change them we will. Let's move on to the next statement:

Life Is Too Short Not to Enjoy Food

I couldn't agree more. I love eating food. Some of my favourite childhood memories involve Sunday lunches at my grandmothers' house. Gran would do a roast lamb with all the trimmings. Or roast pork. Magic! Another great memory is Wednesday night BBQs in the summertime. I can almost smell the charcoal when thinking about it!

We also need to face the fact that there is a huge social aspect to eating. This is not necessarily a bad thing unless we let it be. However, it is really important to be able to attend family gatherings, work functions, drinks and nibbles with friends and so on, with the confidence that you can still enjoy the food without worrying about returning to your bigger days!

Food is also essential for keeping humans alive and we all have preferences in terms of food that tastes good, versus food that we would rather give to the dog.

My main goal with this book is to help you enjoy a wide range of foods, without counting calories or going on some crazy restriction diet that will never last. Another goal I have is to help you see that a lot of the food you think you like, is in fact just a mindset that has been created by eating 'fake' foods that try to mimic the taste of real food. They may taste similar, but the crucial difference is that one is brought to us by mother nature and will sustain, provide energy, and nourish you; while the other is brought to you by people in lab coats and will slowly make you fat, sick, and possibly put you on track for an early grave.

Now I have just hinted on the health risks associated with eating junk. It is really important to clarify that I have no plans to try to lecture you on the dangers of a poor diet. We hear enough about this on the news, TV, social media, and so on. Another reason that I don't intend on harping on about the health risks, is that I think it doesn't make much difference to what people eat!

I used to eat all sorts of rubbish food with full knowledge that it was bad for me. The problem was, I still wanted to eat it, and the health risks (let's face it, unless you choke on a doughnut, bad food usually won't kill you overnight) hardly passed through my mind! If they did, I managed to push them aside fairly smartly, so I could eat the full tub of ice-cream that I had my eyes on!

There is little point in trying to tell anyone to stop eating junk food because it is bad for you. There is evidence of this everywhere. Why do people queue to the door at takeaway chains, when it is well known that stuff is bad for you? Why, on special occasions, do we gift people chocolates or sugary sweets? "Happy birthday, have some type 2 diabetes".

The reason we do so much of this is that we have been brainwashed into thinking this is the food we want. That we deserve this special treat, even though this food is "naughty". Guess what? To still enjoy food, but not eat the garbage that will kill you, we just need to undo the brainwashing.

Okay, great, how do we do that? Well, let's put it another way. Food that tastes like real food, but isn't real food, is not a real taste. What? Does that even make sense? Better break that down. Food that tastes like real food (say, for example, a strawberry milkshake, which funnily enough has a strawberry flavour) but isn't made from strawberries (instead is made from additives, preservatives and chemicals), does not really have a satisfying taste like that of a real strawberry. People in lab coats, working for big corporations, with bad intentions, have tricked you into thinking that you enjoy something that is poison for your body!

Does that click for you? When drinking a soft drink, you are chugging back a sugar-filled nightmare and a fast track to type 2 diabetes. Again, not trying to get you to try and stop drinking the soft drink because it is bad for you. What I am trying to impress on you is the fact that the drink is not really doing anything for you. The way your brain feels when it has a soft drink is an addiction that has been formed after drinking this rubbish over many years. There is a sad state of affairs across the world where children are being diagnosed with type 2 diabetes. This was once an illness thought to only appear in adulthood. I think that soft drink is a major culprit.

Do you think that children naturally want soft drink? Of course not. Babies don't have an intrinsic desire for this rubbish, and neither do older children (or cola-swilling adults for that matter). They have been conditioned by the addictive qualities of the drink and the mass marketing of this rubbish to children. Children got by just fine being nourished by milk and water for thousands of years before soft drinks came along. They (as well as you) certainly don't need it.

Now here is the tricky part. I think that if you took those people in lab coats and sent them back in time, say a thousand years and introduced a readily available soft drink to a hunter-gatherer tribe, they would likely drink it. Think about that for a moment. Imagine healthy and lean tribesmen and tribeswomen with strong, wiry bodies, free of modern illnesses like obesity and type 2 diabetes. Now imagine them finding a never-ending supply of cola, which after an initial period of curiosity and wonder, would be gratefully accepted and guzzled down with great gusto. Food is scarce after all, so this strange, energy-dense drink would be seen as an amazing blessing from their god.

Imagine this tribe after generations of guzzling this cola every day. What might they look like? Yes, that's right, they would probably look like we do today. The results can be viewed easily enough by looking up any indigenous people that you choose. We were once those healthy, lean humans, yet to encounter many modern illnesses. But unlike the tribe in this story, who really wouldn't have to deal with this sugary rubbish being introduced to their diet, we definitely have to deal with it. We need to understand that this fake energy source may give us a quick energy fix, but it is really poisoning our bodies, the effects are just not as fast-acting as some other poisons.

You might be thinking, "I don't care what you say. I enjoy my biscuits and chocolate in the evening time and yes, I know it's not good for me, but I don't care, I'm not giving it up". Now herein lies the great psychology of humans. We can be very closed-minded about this sort of thing. Logic and reasoning go out the window when it comes to emotional attachment. The serial snacker is scared, that's right scared, that they will not be able to handle the torture of "giving up" their 'treats'.

Good news. I am not suggesting you "give up" your 'treats'. I am not suggesting you cut down the amount you eat (within reason, obviously, hot dog eating contestants may need a different plan). Later in the book, I will share ideas on what and when to eat. What I am asking is, you open your mind to the fact that you have been convinced by marketing companies, your family and many others, that you want the sugary, unnatural 'treats'. You have been tricked into putting poison in your body! What's worse, the poison is addictive so reinforcement occurs in your brain, making you want more!

It is super important that you see this for what it is. Let me use a very unlikely scenario as another way to look at this. Step outside of your current perspective and put yourself in the shoes of an alien that is observing humans for the first time. Say two aliens were tasked to study the curious subject of obesity trends in earthlings. The conversation would be something like:

First Alien: "Why are humans getting so fat?"

Second Alien: "Well, from what we can tell they have abandoned their diet, which served them well for thousands of years, for what they eat now."

First alien: "Why would they do that."

Second Alien: "It seems that television told them to, and now they can't stop, even though they are getting sick."

First Alien: "Wait a minute. They know it is killing them and they still do it?"

Second Alien: "Oh yes, we observed one the other day. He was asked to stop, he said that nobody is going to tell him what to do."

First Alien: "Hmm. I don't think we will have much trouble taking over this planet."

The aliens would easily be able to see what is going on here. Humans have been tricked into abandoning their traditional diet and eating patterns, for poison. The not so funny part is, when challenged, fear sets in, and we will defend our right to kill ourselves in this way. I am asking you to take the alien's perspective here. Again, step outside the human point of view and see what has really happened. You don't really want the sugary 'treat', your brain has been tricked into thinking you do!

Anyway, let's get back to the excuse, "Life is too short not to enjoy food". You may think I have become like the food companies and been a bit deceitful here. You may have expected that I was going to say you can still enjoy the foods that you love. Well, you definitely can, but what I want to encourage you to do is change your perception of the food you enjoy. Let me lay out some poisons, sorry, I mean foods: doughnuts, cake, sweets, pies, and bagels. I am not trying to insult your intelligence or accuse you of being untruthful, but again, take the perspective of the alien. Is this really the food you enjoy? Or are you mistaking the addictive qualities for genuine enjoyment?

In my view, you can still enjoy all of the foods that you <u>think</u> you do, but without adding in the poison! This book is not designed to be a recipe book (that masterpiece may be written later), but I will throw in a couple of my favourites in the second section. For example, I love pizza and have a great recipe that allows me to have it without wanting to vomit half an hour later or feeling guilty about eating rubbish. What a concept! Just so you know, other favourites like cake and dessert, fudge, and bread can all still be enjoyed just by swapping out some poison and swapping in some natural ingredients that humans have eaten for thousands of years. In this crazy age of information, getting your hands on such recipes is easy, the trick is, you need to be prepared to do it!

This Is Going Well, but it Won't Last

Have you ever started well on a new way of eating? Or perhaps you have started making a change in another area of your life, such as exercising or budgeting? You began with a hiss and a roar, full of motivation and enthusiasm for the change. "Right world, I am making this happen, time to get out of my way!". However, the whole time there was a lingering doubt at the back of your mind. Thoughts like "This can't be sustainable" or "I know it's only a matter of time before I mess up" might go through your mind. They certainly did for me in the past.

You may have made great progress and lost a lot of weight, only to slowly but surely put it back on again? What happened? Think about the phrase "Is this sustainable?" You will likely have heard this when considering a diet. The theory being, if a diet is too restrictive, it may not be sustainable, meaning you are less likely to stick to it. I think this concept is silly and is holding you back from being able to sort out your weight.

The reason I say this is that when you think that something has to be sustainable, you are inferring that the restrictiveness of the diet determines whether or not you will stick to it. When it should be _you_ that determines whether or not you will stick to it. When you say a diet is not sustainable, to me you are saying, "I know I am weak and will not stick to this". In other words, it is over before it began. You have sabotaged yourself.

Now I know I have said that traditional restrictive dieting isn't the answer, but that is not the point here. Once you have allowed yourself to buy into the unsustainable dogma, you start to look for events or circumstances that allow you to go back to your old ways, while placing the blame elsewhere. Then you can say "See, this always happens to me. Why should I even bother?" When I was a smoker, I would try this ridiculous plan to "only smoke socially". Now quitting smoking is obviously very different from changing what you eat, but stay with me here. The same mentality is applied. I would go for periods of non-smoking and for a while stuck to my plan of only smoking at social events. But predictably, I would find some flimsy reason to go back to smoking all the time. Usually, after a stressful event, such as a tough day at work, I would give in and that would be it!

When this occurred, of course, the external event such as the tough day at work, or some stressful life event, was the "reason" for my failure…it couldn't possibly be me! Again, the reason that I sabotaged myself was that I had not changed the person that I was. I was still stuck with the flawed thinking that I was unable to control my smoking and when I would try to "cut back" or "only smoke on weekends" or some other ridiculous plan, there was one big gaping, glaring problem staring me in the face, that I still could not manage to see…..I had not changed; I was still a smoker! Even when I managed to go two weeks without smoking, I was still a smoker; I just hadn't had one for a while! In my mind, the only way to stop smoking for good was to become a non-smoker. This happens the minute you get it clear in your mind that you are no longer a smoker. The only other thing required is to cut off the supply of nicotine.

The same mentality applies to food. In the case of smoking, you are stopping something that is not required anyway (inhaling smoke into your lungs), while becoming healthy and lean means eating (which humans must do) the good food and not the bad. Different strategies, but the same mentality. Let me explain further. When becoming a lean and healthy person, you have the mindset, that <u>you</u> are in control of your weight and physical being. This means that <u>you</u> are in control of what goes into your mouth and would never place blame on some external person or source for eating something that you shouldn't.

For me, this was another area that needed to change. There was a time when I would eat pretty well when it was easy to, but as soon as I left the comfort of my kitchen, my poor mindset told me that I must eat what was available, which was invariably some processed rubbish. For example, when travelling for work, I used to tell myself that it wasn't my fault that takeaway food all came with fries or bread, or that airport food was so bad for you. I would eat this food, secure in the knowledge that this was not my fault, therefore, not my responsibility- what a load of nonsense. No wonder I couldn't lose weight!

Have you ever done something similar? These days, I look back and see how ridiculous that was. Healthy food can still be an option at the airport, at restaurants, or for take-outs. Again, the mental shift is what is critical here. You need to change (which can happen instantly) from a person that lets small obstacles keep you from your health goals, or you can flip that switch and say, "Damn it, that's enough! No more".

Once you focus on the fact that you are in control, it becomes remarkably easy. I was at dinner recently at a chain type of restaurant, where many of the meals come with fries or bread. Guess what? There were still plenty of meals that didn't include that sort of rubbish. What's more, if you just ask, most places will substitute the fries for a salad. If you are like me and need a decent-sized meal, have another look at the side menu and see what is really there. I discovered this place does a side bowl of pork crackling - beautiful!

Another suggestion is when you are getting a burger, order the bun-less option. They will give you the burger with a bun made from lettuce. I swear, this is true, I prefer my burger this way these days! Once I got the low-quality carbs out of my system, I started to taste the real food much more intensely. One of my favourite home-made meals is burger patties and a big salad that includes pickles and mustard, with cheese, which must be melted on top of the burger! This is heaven as far as I am concerned, with no bread, fries, or sugar-laden sauce!

Sorry, that little burger tangent distracted me from the point I was making. I needed to change my mindset and not make little excuses or stories that I have been telling myself, such as "There is no healthy food at the airport", that was keeping me from eating the way I knew I should. Once you make the mental shift, you are there. All you have to do is not let what other people think throw you off (watch out for people trying to make you feel bad for not eating like them), and see the bad food for what it is - poison. Remember to ask yourself that simple question - "Why would I want to eat poison?"

You will feel an incredible sense of peace, once the inner conflict is resolved and you move from an overweight person, to a healthy and lean one. You will be able to look at situations objectively and instead of feeling tempted to eat the rubbish food, you will feel sorry for other people that are still struggling. It feels like a secret that everyone should know!

What Will Other People Think?

This one can be really challenging. Especially when certain aspects of your culture are based around food and you completely "rock the boat" by daring to be different. You may offend some people. You may get the feeling that they are talking about you behind your back. You may feel obligated to explain yourself.

My extended family is reasonably small, and while we occasionally have social events that are based around food, I am aware that I don't have the same hurdle some of you need to jump over in this regard. If you come from a culture where the extended family gets together and the food is piled up across tables with an expectation that everyone gets a good helping, I can totally see how it would be challenging to go against the grain (again excuse the pun). Some of your family may not take kindly to your choice not to eat the food laid out.

Now I'm sure you will have heard the advice before: "You shouldn't care what other people think". Yeah, that's a load of nonsense! We are social beings. Of course, we care about what other people think. Have you seen Facebook or Instagram? We are posting all sorts of crap and staged photos in an attempt to get attention. We definitely care what other people think! You might find some humans that genuinely don't, they are called psychopaths!

I think it's important to understand why others might feel this way. It seems to me that when someone is doing well, there is an inclination for some of their family and friends to feel a certain level of embarrassment, which can come out as ridicule and unhelpful comments. These people are often stuck in their own story about why their life isn't going the way they want, and will be the first to hand you the chocolate, biscuits, or bottle of cola when you are feeling a bit weak. Don't hang around these people! If you must, you need to take it upon yourself to change and no longer allow their views to influence your success. It is completely normal to care about what they think, but don't let it stop you from achieving your goals!

It's Easy for You, Blah, Blah, Blah

Humans are interesting creatures. We use other people to measure ourselves. Have you ever thought you were doing well in an area of your life, only to find out what another person does and suddenly feel a bit envious? Perhaps you think you are in a reasonable financial position for your age, until you meet someone younger who has a bigger house, better cars, and a higher income than you. How do you feel? I am ashamed to say that I have been envious of these people. As much as I try to work at focusing on how great that is for them, or asking better questions, like "I wonder what I can learn from them?", a part of me wants to make an excuse as to why they are there, and I am not.

Before I catch myself, I will come up with excuses, like "Well I was a solo dad for many years, so I've had bigger financial obligations than them", or "They got lucky and their parents helped them into that business". I am not proud that I sometimes think this way, and I realise it is a reflection on me, that excuses will get me nowhere and my circumstances are for me to control. The reason I raise it, is I believe we allow the same mentality to apply to weight loss or healthy eating.

The other day, I was watching a YouTube video on Michael B Jordan, a celebrity, who has changed his body to a much more muscle-bound, superhero looking physique. The guy had used an intense training programme and had a chef prepare his meals following a strict eating plan. Looking at the changes over time, there was huge progress made. After watching the video, I did a stupid thing and looked at some of the comments. While I am sure that the majority of people that write comments on YouTube are positive and well-meaning (that's sarcasm by the way), there is definitely a selection of negativity and what appears to be some very mean people!

Anyway, while scrolling through, I noticed my fellow viewers writing comments along the lines of "Easy for him, we don't all have a chef to make our meals", or "It's easy when you don't have to work all day". This is a big problem for a lot of people. These are the type of comments that focus on the wrong thing. If you give yourself an excuse for why someone else can succeed and you can't, then you will never become the person you need to be to make the lasting change to your weight. Instead of focusing on what others have, focus on what you have. Ask yourself better questions, like "How can I learn from Michael B Jordan?", and "How can I use what he did to inspire me?".

If, after reading this, your mind still says "Yes, but there are differences in people when it comes to weight loss. Some people can lose weight more easily than others". Here is my response…so what? You shouldn't give a rats' if your friend Katy has a seemingly fast metabolism and can eat whatever she wants without gaining weight. This is not about her, this is about you! If you focus on her and use her circumstances as an excuse or an 'out' for you, you have failed! Don't do it. Whenever such thoughts cross your mind, let them pass you by. Replace them with thoughts like "Won't it be so much sweeter when I am slim, knowing that it doesn't come naturally to me?" or "Screw limitations, I know I am strong, and I can do anything".

Remember earlier in the book when I said that losing weight would not be hard and you won't need to use will power? Please don't think I am now saying that will power and hard work will be required after all. I'm not saying that. What I am definitely saying is, the mentality of focusing on what others have or what you don't have, could sabotage you before you even start. If you have this sort of poor mindset, then I presume that you are also the type that says to themselves, "Well, I will only eat a few of these chocolate biscuits". Keep doing this and you will end up weighing more than you want, and guess what? The old excuses would come out again! "It's okay for you, I've tried everything and the weight just won't come off". Nonsense. I repeat, do not let this happen!

It's My Vice

Okay, now the vice argument is interesting. This is the defensive position that we often take, saying that I am otherwise a good, disciplined person, but in the area of food, "I just don't want to be that way. I can't get by without my packet of chocolate biscuits late at night. It's my vice".

Let's think this one through. This is definitely a mental story we have told ourselves. If you truly believe that eating poorly is your vice and that you simply cannot stop, I would invite you to consider this. When you give yourself an 'out', such as saying "it's my vice", you are again taking away your power to be in control. You know this is all psychological and simply an excuse that you have created, so as not to take responsibility yourself. This is very similar to the saying it is someone else's fault...which you are about to learn.

It's Someone Else's Fault

Do not, I repeat, do not put this book down until you have this clear in your mind. Fault and responsibility are two very different things. If you are you are inclined to, go to YouTube and find Will Smith's explanation of fault vs responsibility. The takeaway message is that while something may not be your fault, it is your responsibility, and blaming others or carrying on like a victim, will not help.

Will uses examples like the child from an abusive household. They cannot help how they were raised and are not at fault. However, it is their responsibility to find a way to be happy in life. If they just use their upbringing as an excuse for not living a happy life, they are trapped as a victim of circumstance.

Think about the obesity issues facing much of the world. Think of your own circumstances. You could build a list of others that you could blame:

1. The government for allowing ridiculous dietary guidelines.
2. Big food companies for advertising junk food aggressively.
3. The wheat industry for large-scale production of cheap and nasty food.
4. Your doctor for still thinking that all cholesterol is bad, no matter what (don't get me started).
5. Your dietitian for still recommending margarine over butter (again, don't get me started).
6. Drug companies for manipulating data and studies to ensure more of their drugs are unnecessarily prescribed.
7. Your well-meaning mother for making sugary deserts.
8. Your well-meaning partner for serving up refined carbs with each meal.

This list could go on and on and everything listed could be true. The problem is (and this is the rub), it is <u>your</u> health at stake here. Therefore, you are the one that is responsible. This may mean that you have to go to some places you don't want to in your mind, but you must, if you want to change.

Let me make this very clear. **If you are overweight, the only person that is <u>responsible</u> is you.**

This is critical to fixing the problem. Is that fair? Not necessarily, but as we all know, life is not fair. If it were, people wouldn't be born into crappy countries, with corrupt governments, where the citizens are forced to live in poverty. If life were fair, people wouldn't get cancer, have life-changing accidents, have children die before them, lose their life savings, and so on. There may be many external factors that can be attributed to the extra pounds around your waist. The factors may not be your fault and they pale in comparison to some circumstances that others are required to endure. But my friend, the extra pounds are definitely your responsibility!

If you need inspiration, the great news is that it is not hard to find examples of people overcoming unfair circumstances to succeed in some area of their life. Just last night, my lovely wife and I were watching one of her favourite TV shows about garden makeovers. The concept is that a worthy person is nominated by their friends or family, and the crew from the show come in and take the neglected garden and transform it. Plenty of room for sappy moments as you learn more about the person nominated. I was only watching it because wifey has it on, I swear!

Anyway, this episode included a guy that had his legs blown off while serving for the British Army in Afghanistan. This would have been a horrific and traumatic event and this guy could have quite easily given up on life or focussed on how unfair this all was. Instead, he focused on helping others, through mentoring soldiers that have suffered from post-traumatic stress disorder. He is married and has a little boy. Seems like a top bloke.

The reason I mention him is that his amazing outlook and the way he had taken an unfair situation and turned it into a positive story, are great examples that we can all follow when shedding the victim mentality and focusing on what you can control. You may have a slower metabolism, bad genes, or a solid build, but that cannot stop you from living a healthy and happy life. Well, it can if you let it. I am saying make like the soldier with no legs and say, "stuff it, I'm not going to wallow in this and feel sorry for myself. I can overcome any stupid circumstance that life throws at me". "F%&k you world, I'm being trim and healthy!"

Fat Shaming

Okay, we know that fat-shaming is a thing. Some people take perverse pleasure in making fun of others that are overweight and ridiculing them with lines, such as "Can't you control yourself?", or generalisations like "Fat people are lazy". Now let me be clear, the people that fat shame are only letting their feelings of insecurity be evident for the world to see. Sometimes, it is under the guise of "only out of concern for your health" while other times, it is a case of blatantly being mean. Either way, you should feel sorry for the person doing the fat-shaming, as you can rest assured, they have their own issues to deal with, and I can guarantee they are not truly happy in life. Also, as I have gotten older, I have come to believe more that there are some external factors at play. Whether you call it Karma, or the Universe, or something else, I'm believing more and more, that what you put out there comes back to you, so these people may be in for a taste of their own medicine.

Now, this is the really important part. Fat people <u>should</u> feel ashamed. Let me explain. What I mean is that a fat person that would rather defend their right to be fat, than actually try to change and lose weight, should feel very ashamed of the ridiculous position they have taken. Come to think of it, ashamed is the wrong word. Fat people that defend their right to be fat and seek the support of the PC brigade to stop people fat-shaming, should feel stupid! If you do this, you are worried about external factors and defending the wrong thing! Obesity is a huge (pun intended) health problem, and we have a huge problem in the way we treat food and accept obesity in our culture. Defending your right to be big, is no different from a smoker defending their right to kill themselves via cigarettes. You can focus on defending that right and trying to control how others view you, or you can actually take some action, and sort out your health!

Speaking of smokers, can you imagine if we treated smoking the way we do bad food? On social occasions, people would be offered cigarettes and made to feel bad if they declined. "I have been slaving over the cigarettes all day, at least have a few". If you read the ingredients, you would find cigarettes to be in everything! You would feel pressured to have cigarettes because they advertise on TV all the time and "That's what you do when the family gets together, we all share a bunch of cigarettes".

This seems crazy, but think about the harm that obesity is doing to people. We have come a long way with smoking. People think nothing of the fact that smoking is bad for you, and believe me, as a former smoker, I know that my fellow citizens are happy to let smokers know that it is bad for their health. Why don't we do the same for eating junk food? Perhaps if you try to buy a bottle of fizzy drink and a bag of chips at the supermarket, you should be asked if you know that it is bad for you? Would you be offended? You shouldn't be, you know it is!

I doubt that our attitude to junk food and smoking will ever align, but the point should not be overlooked; both are terrible for your health. You should not confuse the fact that yes, you should not be fat-shamed and you should feel confident in yourself, with the fact that you <u>do</u> need to stop eating food that is slowly killing you. I think now is a good time to reiterate two things.

1 -   If you're reading this and think to yourself, I don't care if I am big, I am happy and don't need to lose weight. Great! I would again suggest you stop reading, as this book isn't for you! Go live a happy life the way you are.

2 -   If you are offended by people that comment on your weight, you may need to consider that you do need to lose weight, for the sake of your health – hopefully, that is why you are reading this book.

What About Physical Addiction?

Is it possible to have a physical addiction to food? Probably. Is it possible to have a psychological disorder that compels you to eat junk food without the conscious ability to stop? Well, I am sure this is possible, but I would imagine that genuine addiction being the problem is pretty unlikely. If you genuinely believe you have such a disorder, I suggest you consult a doctor and arrange specialist treatment.

Otherwise, addiction is just another story we tell ourselves to try and take away accountability for our own actions. The solution to this, as I suspect you would have guessed by now, is to change and become a person that no longer eats junk food.

Genetics

It's my genes man. Easy for me with my European genetics and skinny legs to drop weight. What about those that are naturally big? This is a completely fair question. We do come in all shapes and sizes, and some people are built bigger than others and are prone to weight gain.

I like to go to the gym and lift weights. Each visit I work my skinny, pale legs like crazy, completely envious that some other guys do nothing and are blessed with much more shapely calves! We are all put together differently. Does this mean if you are naturally big you should just give up on reaching a healthy weight? Of course not!

Is it realistic that one of my friends from the Pacific Islands, from a lineage of athletic, strong, warrior people, who naturally weighs around 100kg (220 pounds) tries to get down to my weight? No way! That would be called starvation. However, if that is you, and you know that mixed in with the truth that you are naturally big, is the just as true point that you are bigger than you should be, then you can't use your genetics as an excuse.

When I got a shock at the doctor's a few years back, I weighed 83kg (183 pounds). This was lighter than any player in the All Blacks rugby team. The problem was, for my body type, it was overweight. Whenever I talk about a lean and healthy weight in this book, I mean whatever lean and healthy is for you. The number on the scales will be different for everyone. What you can measure is your blood-pressure lowering, and your energy levels increasing!

Part Two - Okay, so Now What?

What to eat? Take the science with a grain of salt (wait, are grains good or bad for you? What about salt?). Let's try common sense instead.

Studies and Science

Want to get confused? Just deep dive into weight loss online. You will find information to support you, and information that conflicts with just about any way of eating. Another place is in media headlines. There is so much information in our faces. There is also the influence of food companies and just like big tobacco influenced policy and studies, big food and drug companies have a vested interest in keeping us eating the way we do.

You will see headlines that tell you things like:

1. "Study shows that eggs may kill".
2. "Study shows that eggs may be good for you".
3. "Study shows a glass of red wine a day may have health benefits".
4. "Study links wine to cancer".
5. "Study links red meat to cancer".
6. "Saturated fat not so bad after all?".

In this book, I have deliberately steered clear of science or citing studies. When trying to work out what food I should eat, and considering the health impacts, my rule of thumb is this: does it make sense to me? An example is, should we eat margarine or butter? Hmm, let me look at the ingredients:

Butter
Cream.
Salt.

Margarine

A big long list of words, many of which I don't understand!

I am sure you will find studies that will tell you margarine is better than butter, and vice versa. For me, I understand the ingredients in butter, and I don't understand the ingredients in margarine. I also know that humans have eaten butter for hundreds of years, while margarine was invented in a lab by accident. If you were to place a tub of margarine and butter on a table outside and come back in a few days, you will find that insects and animals have been into the butter, but left the margarine alone! You may not like saturated fat or the fact that it is an animal product. Compared with margarine, I will take my chances with butter as my spread of choice!

Another issue with science is that it is all theoretical, until it is actually tried by you. Guess what, people are different! Eating a certain way may be fine for you, while it makes another person fat. I know that when people that live to 100 years old have been asked what they eat, there was a huge variance. Many eat meat, many drink coffee, some drink alcohol, some don't. I know of ninety-plus-year-olds that have enjoyed meat and whiskey every day for most of their lives! Does this mean it will work for you? You can't really know that, because these are other people, not you!

Genetics has to play a part here, too. Have you noticed that in many countries where the Western diet has been introduced, the indigenous people of that land end up with health markers that are much worse than the Westerners? Why would this be? I don't need a study to tell me that the indigenous people, who for thousands of years lived off the diet that their environment provided, would then struggle to adapt to a diet containing heavily-processed food, sugars, and vegetable oils. Common sense tells me their bodies would revolt!

People of Asian descent have lived for thousands of years on rice and a relatively high carbohydrate diet. The eye test tells me that people of this genetic makeup manage to cope well with this diet and in general do not become fat eating this way. However, I know that if you placed me on this diet, I would definitely put on weight! How do I know this? The scales tell me when I check after eating this food for a while.

When you take the people native to Alaska and place them on the standard American diet, they become sick. If they eat their traditional diet high in omega-three fatty acids from fish such as salmon, they thrive, and their health improves. Again, there is no need for a study to tell me this, just common sense.

Over in the Middle East, children are showing signs of obesity at an alarming rate. I wonder why? I'm kidding. Unfortunately, the answer is obvious. The all-consuming Western diet has made its way over. Take-away chains have moved in, and in the hot climate, soft drink is being guzzled by fat children! If these children drank water and ate more along the lines of hummus and falafel, I'm pretty confident they would be in much better shape.

'Diets' You May Have Tried in the Past

Have you tried this before? Get yourself motivated to lose some weight and use what seems like a sensible approach - count calories, track your food, and weigh yourself daily. This approach makes sense, as it is in line with the first rule of thermodynamics: energy in equals energy out. All you need to do is carefully track everything, and let solid science do the rest. Right? Well, in my experience, wrong!

If you want to learn more about this, I suggest reading some of the works of Gary Taubes. What I will say on the subject is this. If controlling weight were a simple case of calories in/calories out, our weight would fluctuate like crazy. Think about it for a moment. Let's say, to maintain your weight, you need to eat an average of 2000 calories per day. How carefully would you need to track calories to achieve this? Given there are, say, 100 calories in a banana, if you accidentally ate two bananas more than you were supposed to, in theory, you would be 10% over your calorie limit for the day. Or if you went four over, that would be 20%, etc., and your weight would increase accordingly.

If you adopted the 2000 calorie per day "break-even" limit, this would mean you need to eat exactly 730,000 calories in a year. Do you really think anyone, short of being an incredibly strict (and boring) type, that cooks and weighs all of their own food, would be able to eat the exact number of calories required to, in theory, maintain their weight? I would suggest this is one of the silliest things I have ever heard, and that the average person would have no clue how many calories they eat in a day, let alone a year! "Would you like to go out for a beer?", "No sorry, I am at my caloric limit for the day"...give me a break! Also, think about the times you have eaten lots, or eaten less than normal. Do you notice a predictable correlation with your weight? Would you even know how many calories you have consumed? Some people maintain their high school weight their whole lives. Do you think they are have tracked and consumed the same number of calories every year? Of course not!

Have you ever watched that show, 'The Biggest Loser'? These poor people are subjected to crazy, low-calorie diets, and then forced into extreme exercise to try to lose weight. Do they lose weight? Absolutely. However, have you also noticed that despite regulating what they eat and the amount of exercise they do, when it comes to the weigh-in, the amount of weight loss is notoriously unpredictable? In fact, some weeks when they weigh-in, they actually gain weight, despite exercising like crazy! Why would that be? If using the science of calories in/calories out, it should be very easy to predict the amount of weight a person would lose. The problem is, there is way more to it than that!

Now in spite of this, calorie counting can work. There are diets out there that use point systems, where you are allowed to eat foods up to a certain value each day. Some people make this work. I tried this for a while myself. I kept a log and wrote down everything that I ate for a few months. I started weighing my food and rationing what I could have. Sound like fun? Of course not!

This silly arrangement did work for me, but there were three major problems:

1. I couldn't seem to lose as much weight as I thought I would.
2. Because I couldn't eat as much as I wanted to, I was hungry a lot!
3. I did not want to write down and count calories for the rest of my life!

With these problems outweighing (pun intended) the benefits I felt I was receiving, I stopped counting calories, and put back all the weight I had lost. You could definitely say that I could have tried harder here, and that if I really wanted it, I could have stuck to this diet. The problem was, I didn't want to. The few kilograms of weight loss just weren't enough bang for my buck to be taking out a set of scales every time I make a meal! This was not the answer!

I'm pretty confident that early humans (or all other animals that regulate their weight with no trouble) would never try to count calories. The human body is far more complicated, with hormones, genetics, and all sorts of other factors making up the weight regulation. Now, how to lose weight is not complicated, but in my humble opinion, calorie counting is not the long-term answer. Plus, aside from the truly obsessives among us, who would want to bloody do that?!

What Should You Eat?

Okay, most of this book focused on the 'why'. I have explained to you that there is little point starting if you haven't changed your mindset and become a lean and healthy person (that happens when you decide to be one, not when you change what you eat). We have looked at the great tricks that have been played, and the brainwashing that has occurred. I go back to the quote "Happy birthday, here's some type 2 diabetes".

Now that you have changed, (if you haven't quite gotten there, go back and read part one again), we can look at the 'how'. Good news, this is the easy part. You already know the food that you should eat. It is just a matter of making sure it is clear in your mind, so you don't get confused when your work colleagues are trying to make you feel bad about not eating the rubbish food served at work functions.

DIETS ARE STUPID!

Here are two lists. Can you tell me which is the bad one?

List 1
1. Bagels.
2. Chocolate biscuits.
3. Cookies.
4. Bread.
5. Pasta.
6. Chips.
7. Slice of pie.
8. Cake.
9. Soft drink.

List 2
1. Eggs.
2. Vegetables.
3. Meat.
4. Fish.
5. Butter.
6. Nuts.

Now look at these two lists and I am sure you can see immediately that I am suggesting List 1 is bad. What about List 2? Do you agree that the food listed here are good? I'm not going to tell you what you should eat, but I would invite you to consider adopting my rule of thumb: if it is normally food found in nature and lower in carbohydrates, then I eat it most of the time. If it is a natural food, but high in carbs (fruit for instance), you might want to eat this less frequently. If it is not natural food, such as processed sugar, vegetable oil, margarine, packaged meals, or floury baked goods, I avoid it wherever possible. Simple.

But should I eat carbs? Low fat? High fat? What about veganism? Let me elaborate here. I don't like labelling "diet", or making huge restrictions, as they can set you up to fail. For me, generally eating in a lowish-carb way suits me best, and very easily allows me to control my weight. However, for you, eating a traditional Chinese type of diet high in fish and rice might do the trick. Or if you prefer not to eat animal products, eating a vegan diet could be the option for you. You may wish to eat a combination of these!

With any way of eating, what I would stress is that being the lean and healthy person you have become, you no longer feel the need to eat the rubbish that previously caused your weight gain. So, if you eat a vegan diet, this would include excellent food like fresh vegetables, beans, nuts, or healthy plant-based meat substitutes (be careful with meat substitutes, they can be full of additives). Just to be clear, your vegan eating would not be made up of cola, chips, and white bread! That is bad food, and you know it!

To me, deciding what to eat is simple. The 'food' on List 1 has not been around for thousands of years, and those in List 2 have (okay maybe some, dairy hasn't; but animals have, and dairy comes from them, right?). Think about that. A bagel, for instance, is made up of wheat flour and other nasties. Wheat flour is a refined carbohydrate that raises blood sugar levels. You will also find that the modern wheat plant has been modified over the years, and is completely different to what was consumed thousands of years ago. You may be sceptical about this. I am not a wheat expert (if you would like more info on this, go and read the book, *Wheat Belly* by William Davis), but I do know that once this sort of food was removed from my diet, the weight fell off and my stomach calmed down. I would, therefore, argue that you shouldn't eat a wheat flour bagel...ever.

If you really wanted a bagel, do a quick Google search for "low carb bagel recipe", or "no wheat bagel recipe", and you will find an alternative with instructional videos! This means that you can easily avoid the wheat flour bagel. The question goes back to, have you changed the person that you are, so as you don't want the wheat flour bagel? Are you now someone that is prepared to make it yourself, rather than buy the cheap rubbish that is available at the supermarkets? Would a lean and healthy person even want to eat the supermarket bagel?

You might be thinking, "but I have seen lean people eating bagels, I don't want to give them up". I would refer you back to the section, "It's easy for you, blah blah blah". You would be right, but there is a big difference, they are lean, you are not! That may sound a bit harsh, but it is important to remember that we are changing you, not worrying about the fact that your friend Johnny can eat McDonald's three times per week and never put on weight. Excuse the language, but F&*k Johnny! This is about you and your health. You need to see the food for the poison it is, then the lean and healthy you can come out!

What about chocolate biscuits? I used to love these after dinner while watching TV! Well, have a look at the back of the packet and read the ingredients. Actually, if you want to get depressed, do this with everything that you are pondering on eating. Back to the biscuits. While writing this, I checked in our cupboards and there was a packet (I wouldn't touch them but my lovely, pregnant at the time, wife said she needed them!). Here is the list of ingredients:

Wheat flour.
Sugar.
Vegetable fat [antioxidant (307b : SOY)].

45

Mild solids.
Cocoa butter.
Cocoa mass.
Invert syrup.
Golden syrup.
Emulsifiers (Soy Lecithin, 476).
Salt.
Raising agents (Baking Soda 450).
Natural flavours.
Natural colour (Annatto Extracts)

Back when I did eat this sort of rubbish, did the chubbier version of me know that this food was bad for my health? Of course. I am fairly confident that you would already know that this list of ingredients is terrible for you. Unfortunately, it is easy to put this out of your mind when you are in denial and trapped in the mindset of a heavier person. Once the change in mindset occurs, you will not want to eat this sort of rubbish.

The excellent news is that we are stupidly lucky to live in this day and age where we can simply Google search recipes for chocolate biscuits, if that is what you really want to eat. Actually, below is a list of ingredients from the first Google search I entered for healthy chocolate biscuits. I previously hadn't tried these, but for research purposes, I gave them a shot, and can confirm that they are top-notch!

Spelt flour.
Raw cocoa powder.
Baking powder.
Baking soda.
Salt.
Raw honey.
Dark chocolate.

Organic butter.
Pure vanilla extract.
Organic eggs.
Milk.

Now, I would suggest that if you really wanted to eat chocolate biscuits, the second list of ingredients looks to me to be a much better option! Remember the rule of thumb, is it made it in nature?

Just out of interest, scanning the ingredients in List 1, I didn't know what several of them were. For the fun of it, I Googled soy lecithin, 476. Remember how I said I would avoid getting into citing studies, as they can be so conflicting and it is hard to know if the information can be relied upon? A quick Google search shows confusing results, and the information on soy lecithin 476, is not easy to quickly understand at first glance. I have taken the approach that if the ingredients have things like this that I don't understand, then I don't eat them. I doubt that I will regret not having enough soy lecithin 476 in my diet.

What Do I Eat?

As I have already mentioned, for me, lowering the carbohydrates works. Did you know that your body can burn ketones for energy? This occurs when you have used up your body's glycogen stores. If you read about lower-carb eating, you will soon start to see the often-confusing term ketogenic diet, or "keto" diet. There is a difference between low carb and keto. Essentially, the keto diet is even more restrictive on carbohydrates, and requires an even higher portion of your calories from fat, than the regular low carb diet. Like low carb on steroids perhaps.

Personally, I eat a lower carb-ish diet, most of the time. Though, while editing this book, I have been eating oatmeal a lot lately. Please remember, when I say diet, I mean it in the sense of the word that indicates what my food is made up of. Just like a Koala bear has a diet of eucalyptus leaves, I am using the word diet to mean the make-up of the food I eat, not the other use of the word, you know, like a person restricting themselves and 'dieting' against their wishes.

Eating low a lower carb-ish diet is not something I do while actually wanting to eat rice, bread, and pasta. The way I eat is the way I want to eat. For me, the food I eat keeps my weight where I want it, my digestive system happy (IBS issues gone), and the food tastes good! One of the reasons that this way of eating works for me, is that there are periods of ketosis where my body is using fat for fuel. How do I know this? I don't. I have never checked to see if I am in ketosis. I simply have tracked my weight when eating different ways, and I am very confident that the 12 kgs (26 pounds) I have lost and kept off, is not an accident nor a coincidence.

However, please don't think I am suggesting you should eat this way. If you want to eat bananas, brown rice, and starchy vegetables, I am sure you can still lose weight. It is the removal of the rubbish food that counts. As an example, another (extreme) option is the carnivore diet. People are reporting curing all sorts of ailments by switching to eating meat only. While this doesn't sound appealing to me, and I am not suggesting you need to adopt such an extreme approach, at the end of the day, all of these ways of eating have a common theme, real food that humans are supposed to eat!

I was watching an interesting explanation on YouTube recently of why seemingly contrasting ways of eating can all lead to improvements in the health markers of those that adopt these different ways of eating. They have all cut out refined carbohydrates, vegetable oils, processed sugars, and high fructose corn syrup. Once you make this change, you will be amazed at how the weight just falls off, and your overall health improves.

One day, as an experiment, I may try a month on the carnivore diet or veganism for a month or two, just for fun. I am confident that my weight would remain healthy. This is the great thing about it, you should not need to worry about being restricted. There is such an amazing array of food out there, fantastic spices and flavours brought to us by mother nature, that once you remember what real food tastes like, you will not feel any desire to eat the processed poison that lines our supermarket shelves!

Intermittent Fasting - How to Really Get the Weight Loss Going

Now that you have changed to the type of person that doesn't eat rubbish, it won't take long to see changes in your weight. Once you cut off the supply of bad food that spikes insulin and is converted to fat, you will be amazed at the ease in which your body starts to drop the weight off. This is great, and by changing, you have potentially added years to your life.

If you would like to take this change even further, and in line with using common sense and getting back to what humans used to do, I would like to invite you to consider intermittent fasting. You may already be familiar with this phrase and have your own thoughts on this, but if you have come this far in the book, I would ask that you hear me out on this one.

Think about humans thousands of years ago (you know before colonials were converting natives to their way of life). These people didn't have convenience food, refrigerators, or the ability to have food delivered to them with a few taps on their phone. Food was eaten when available. This would have meant that there were periods when there was no food to be eaten (sometimes days at a time). It makes complete sense to me that humans are quite capable of going for significant periods without eating. If I were picking how earlier humans used to eat, I would imagine that the three meals a day paradigm would simply not have worked. If you were hunting meat and didn't have a way to store it, feasting when possible, followed by periods of fasting, would most likely be how things were done. Imagine the satisfying feeling of eating all those calories from fat!

The reason that I raise this, is common sense tells me that the human body is likely to be quite adaptable to periods of fasting, using fat for fuel. Hunger is an inherent way for the brain to know to seek food, but imagine if there is no food forthcoming. Early humans couldn't dial for a Pizza! If there was no food, they had to go without, until they could find or catch something. The hunger pangs don't last. The body tells you that food is required, but once it realises that food isn't coming, the hunger passes, and the body uses fat reserves for fuel.

Okay, but why do it? Well, the theory here is that the body does a lot of cool stuff when going for significant periods without food. The body can burn glucose for energy (which is what happens when you eat carbohydrates), or once the glucose supply is exhausted, the body can burn ketones. Ketone bodies are burned by your body when you reduce the carbohydrates in your diet past a threshold, where your body switches fuel sources. Or if you simply stop eating for long enough. Burning ketones means you are burning fat. Burning fat is why you are reading this book!

Now ketosis is a subject where you can do your own research and due diligence. You are an adult and can make your own decisions. What I want to talk about here is my personal experience with intermittent fasting (let's use IF for short). IF was something I have been aware of for many years and had always been intrigued by. I liked the idea of the health benefits attained by giving your body a break from digesting food. One of the reasons that I did not try it sooner was that I loved eating regularly, or at least I thought I did. I was a child of "breakfast is the most important meal of the day" dogma. In my old way of thinking, in asking me to miss a meal, you may as well ask me to go walk in traffic!

I distinctly remember a trip to Melbourne a few years back. I was staying with friends and we decided to go out for breakfast one morning. Unfortunately, the place was full and we were required to wait outside before we could be seated. In my mind, this was one of the worst mornings of my life, I was so hungry! My friends thought it was hilarious how "hangry" I became as the morning went on, without any sign of us being seated! I was certainly losing all patience and perspective, consumed by the thought of getting food. This seems ridiculous to me now, but back then, I genuinely felt I couldn't possibly go all morning without eating and still function.

Anyway, it was this type of thinking that put me off ever trying IF. However, more recently, with changing how I view food, I became curious about this again. I spoke with a friend of mine that came to my wedding and was looking really trim. "What have you been doing to get so trim mate?" I asked him. He put it down to IF. "I just don't eat until 1 pm. I cheat on it all the time" was his simple approach to this way of eating. That didn't sound too hard.

Okay, you may already know that there are many different approaches to choose from with IF. I will address that stuff soon, but first, let me share what I did. So, after changing the food I eat, cutting out the bread, pasta, sugar, empty carbs, and vegetable oils, the weight was definitely coming down, which was great. I really wanted to get down to my high school weight of 75kg (165 pounds) but after the initial burst of weight loss, I seemed to hover around 76kg, which was still really good for me, but I wanted more!

I decided I would add IF to my life, just to see what happened. I was prepared to approach this with an open mind, and was definitely not attached to the success or failure of IF. I really just wanted to be able to say I have tried it properly. If it wasn't for me, that would be fine too. Well, after a few short weeks, I was converted in terms of the results. I was able to sail past the 75kg (165 pounds), first into the 74s, then 73, and the next time I checked the scales, I was 71.9kg (158 pounds)! I was stunned. My pants no longer fit, people commented on how much weight I had lost, and I had to go and have my wedding ring re-sized to stop it falling off my skinny finger, and had to have all of my pants for work taken in. It almost felt like I cheated!

I was still eating (healthy) deserts, having a beer if I felt like it, and we were still eating out as a family when we wanted to! Isn't losing weight meant to be torture? In my experience, well, not really! It seems to me that once you get to that sweet spot where you know to eat good food, are prepared to think ahead of situations where you need to plan your food and finally to eat within a shorter window, the weight loss is really easy!

What did I do specifically? Here is why it felt like I cheated. I ate the same amount of food I was eating before IF, I just changed <u>when</u> I ate it. Let me repeat that, I ate the same <u>amount</u> of food! **<u>Before</u> IF, my typical meals and time on a workday would be something like this:**

6.30 am   A green smoothie with coconut cream, almonds and maybe protein powder.
10.00 am   A handful of almonds.
12.00 pm   A big salad with four boiled eggs.
7.00 pm   Meat and vegetables.
8.00 pm   A sugar-free dessert (e.g., cream and keto cookies, or berries and cream)

<u>Now</u>, it would look something like this:

1.00 pm   A green smoothie with coconut cream, almonds, and maybe protein powder.
2.30 pm   A big salad with four boiled eggs.
4.00 pm   A handful of almonds.
7.00 pm   Meat and vegetables.
8.00 pm   A sugar-free dessert (e.g. cream and keto cookies).

All I have changed is that I eat my food within an 8-hour window. It is very simple to follow. I just aim not to eat until 12 pm or after 8 pm. That's it!

So why did I lose weight, while still eating the same food? Well evidently, when my body goes without food for long enough, it uses stored fat for fuel. Imagine the hunter-gatherers that humans once were, foraging for food wherever they could, and hanging out for their next big catch of meat (and all the fat it would provide). Whoever designed humans was smart enough to know that our bodies would go for long periods without food, and while we would have a powerful built-in reminder to get more food (i.e. hunger), ultimately, if nothing were available, our clever bodies could burn fat in the interim. It makes sense to me!

Will your body burn fat using this same eating window? There is only one way to find out. I mentioned that there are different approaches to IF. Think about the term intermittent fasting. It is pretty loose. How often is intermittent and how long is fasting? By this definition, you could say that everyone fasts for a certain period each day when they go to sleep. So, it seems that to be effective, there needs to be longer fasting, over and above the eight odd hours of sleep that most people have (and therefore, presumably, don't eat).

The purpose of this book is not to try and sell you IF. It has worked really well for me, and has been an easy way to keep my weight down. You may think, "Stuff that! I love my breakfast too much" or "I don't want to go without food for that long". Fair enough! No one is forcing you to do this, and there are plenty of lean and healthy people that eat breakfast every day! IF is just another tool you can place in the toolbox that is available for you at any time.

If you decide to give this a go, here are a few feeding windows to consider: As already mentioned, I do an eight-hour feeding window of about 12 pm to 8 pm. This could be moved around to suit your lifestyle and time of day that you prefer to eat, e.g., 6 am to 2 pm. Other people will eat normally five days per week, and fast for two days (some will allow up to 500 calories on the two days). Some people will fast for 3-10 days at a time once a year (or more).

There is science behind all of this, but basically, if you can find a period of fasting that allows your body to burn fat more easily, then you are good. If you happen to be a super trim person that does not have any weight issues, you probably don't need to think about IF (although I am told there are many other health benefits to giving your digestive system long breaks). But then again, if you were super trim, you probably wouldn't be reading this book to begin with!

Personally, I find 12 pm to 8 pm works in with my life, and allows me to have a pretty normal social life in terms of eating. Do I ever eat outside this window? Absolutely. If wifey wants to go out for breakfast on a Sunday, I don't tell her I can't, just because I don't usually eat until 12 pm! Again, think about early humans, they would have eaten when food was available, not by using an IF protocol and counting the hours since they last ate. The reason that modern humans need to put parameters in place is that we have food in abundance, which has led to us grazing often. A day where I eat breakfast is not going to ruin this way of eating. If you feel like you need to sacrifice your social life to keep eating this way, you may have chosen the wrong method!

But is it hard to go that long without food? As much as I would love to say that I found it easy, I won't kid you, I found it to be really tough! For me, I would have days where I felt okay not having breakfast, and while I had hunger pangs, I could drink water, keep busy and "get through" to 12 pm. Other days, I was in a bad way. I noticed that if I felt like I didn't sleep enough the night before, my body seemed to want lots of energy, I would feel faint and as if there was no possible way I could hold out so long.

Right from the start, I was getting results, but thought, "can I actually do this? I feel like crap!". I found myself using the dreaded will power to get me through each morning without food. This did not seem like it could work long term. Surely, I would find a way to go back to my old eating ways.

Watch out for this. Hopefully you, ya lucky duck, are one of the many that I have read about that adapt easily after a few days (some people say they were never a breakfast person anyway, and IF came super easy to them). The experience I had seems to be not as common, and there are definitely a few suggested remedies if you are experiencing the horrible hunger pangs and very unhappy mornings that I was having. Do stick with it. You know, nothing worth doing is easy and all that!

One option is to look at what you are eating. Now, I maintain that this book is not about what macronutrient ratio you should eat. How much of your diet comes from fat, protein, and carbs was not something that early humans would have worried about, and across the planet, the food available would have determined the ratio of these "macros". To me, this means that we likely can eat quite different ratios and get on just fine.

However, in saying that, I am told that a diet higher in fat is likely to be effective when combined with IF. I would encourage you to do your own reading on this before starting, but basically, if you eat a ketogenic diet (about 80% fat), your body is running on ketones for fuel, which is what your body switches to at some point when you fast. The idea here is that this is much more stable and easier for your body to deal with when you go from eating to fasting. You don't get the large spikes in insulin and feelings of "starvation" associated with eating carbohydrates. This might be an option for you.

You can also try drinking coffee, though there is some debate as to whether you are truly fasting when drinking coffee (I do and it seems to work for me). Lots of water is recommended, and you could also try apple cider vinegar. Easing into your eating window is also an option. Maybe have breakfast at 10 am for a month and see how you go with that, before pushing it out to 12 pm.

When I was researching the topic of IF, it seemed that most people would feel hungry for the first few days, maybe even a week, then their body would adjust and they wouldn't feel the hunger pangs. This was not the case for me! I finally felt better after about 10 weeks, that's right, 10 freaking weeks before I felt like I was used to the change! If you are lucky enough to adjust quickly, great, but be prepared for a long period of adjustment, just in case.

Now, I'll apologise in advance for writing about this. Hopefully, you aren't in the middle of dinner while reading this! Another side effect of IF that I didn't think about beforehand, was diarrhoea. Without getting too far into the gory details, I found that after eating nothing until lunchtime when I would eat a substantial meal, within about an hour, I would need to rush to the bathroom! Just a lovely experience when you work in an office! What was the problem? Well, the food I was eating was no different from my normal fare. I believe that my body was struggling to digest such a large meal so quickly on an empty stomach. Digestive distress was the result. Yay!

This was easily remedied though, by breaking my fast with what I usually eat, but in a much smaller serving, followed by another small meal a few hours later (essentially taking my big meal, and making two smaller meals out of it). I am also told that people adapting to saturated fat in their diet can experience similar symptoms, due to the bile that is created. If this is the case, you may need to cut back on the fat, and ease your body into it more slowly.

Wait, didn't I just say that a high-fat diet may be easier when adjusting to IF? Now I am saying to reduce the fat as it could be too much? Yep, sorry about that, but you will have to try for yourself and figure out what works for you. Everyone is different.

Some Favourite Recipes

I am not a master chef and this is not a cookbook, but on my food journey, I have found some great alternative recipes that allow me to eat the way I want to, while still eating the foods I love. Here's a few gems:

Lower Carb Pizza

You may have come across the cauliflower version of a low carb pizza. While healthy, I didn't find the texture of the base very satisfying. To me, Pizza should be somewhat crispy. Try this bad boy:

Base
1 egg.
2 cups mozzarella cheese (slightly melted).
1 cup almond flour.
2 tablespoons cream cheese.

Topping
Pizza sauce (check the ingredients and try to get one that isn't full of sugar, or make your own).
Baby spinach.
Ham (real ham off the bone).
Cheese.
Peppers.
Italian herbs.
Whatever else you like that is real food!

Mix the base ingredients in a bowl. Then take parchment paper, and place over your pizza tray and scoop the mixture onto the middle of the tray. Take a second piece of parchment paper and place it on top of the mixture, and roll the dough until flat and roughly the size of the tray. Slowly peel off the top piece of parchment paper, and place the base in the oven at 200 degrees Celsius (or 392 degrees Fahrenheit) for 15 minutes, or until golden brown. You will need to flip the base over, remove the second piece of parchment paper, and brown the underside. I usually bake for 15 minutes then grill both sides, as I like a crispy base.

Remove from the oven and add your toppings as desired. Return to oven for a further 5-10 minutes until the cheese is melted and the toppings cooked to your satisfaction. Enjoy!

Chocolate Chip Cookies
½ cup of coconut flour.
100 grams of butter (soft).
2 eggs.
½ teaspoon of baking power.
2 teaspoons vanilla essence.
4-6 squares of 95% dark chocolate cut into chocolate chips.
1 tablespoon of honey (or low carb sweetener such as Stevia if preferred).

Mix well together in a bowl and separate into 10-12 biscuits on a banking tray (lined with parchment paper or grease with butter first). Bake for approximately 12 minutes at 180 degrees Celsius (356 degrees Fahrenheit).

Pancakes
This is probably my favourite and so easy!
4 eggs.
2 tablespoons cream cheese.
½ cup almond flour.

Toss the ingredients into a blender and blend until well mixed. Then cook in a pan just like regular pancakes. I like them with peanut butter or whipped cream!

Super Easy Banana Bread
2 eggs.
2 very ripe bananas.
1 teaspoon of baking powder.
1 and ¾ cups of almond flour (or almond meal).
¼ cup olive oil.
 Optional- add honey or Stevia as desired to sweeten.

I can do this one in my sleep now. There are other recipes around with more ingredients, but I like this simple one. Mix the ingredients in a bowl. Take a bread tin and line with parchment paper, and throw it in the oven at 180 degrees Celsius (356 degrees Fahrenheit) for 50-60 mins. Check that it is cooked by inserting a thin knife into the middle, and if you can pull it out with nothing stuck to it, it is done. If you prefer a sweeter bread, add a few tablespoons of honey to the mixture.

Stop Seeking Comfort

I debated where to put this section. While I wanted you to change your mindset as you read this book, I felt that this concept should be explained towards the end, with the hope that you would be able to lean on it in times where you are struggling or questioning why you are doing this.

Back at the start of this book, I said that once you change your mindset, it would be easy. I maintain that this is true, and that once you have made the mental shift, becoming a trim and healthy person will come without dieting or feelings of deprivation. One part of the change in mindset that I have not fully explained until now, is that you need to change your view on being uncomfortable.

When I say this, I don't mean that you should feel uncomfortable with the food that you eat to the extent that you feel deprived. If that is the case, then this book hasn't helped you, and I have failed! What I mean is that in so many aspects of our lives, we seek comfort at every opportunity. This makes sense from an evolutionary perspective. Humans naturally seek shelter, warmth, the safety of the group, etc. The problem is that in this modern world, we are seeking out comfort in all areas of our lives, and we have missed the point on the reason we have the privilege of living on planet earth.

If you ask most people what their goals are in life, many will say they don't know. The ones that do answer will say things like, to not have to work, or to be rich. I would argue that goals such as this will not make you happy. Imagine if you were to just not work...what would you do all day? I am not saying that it wouldn't be fun for a while, but unless you developed a passionate pursuit for you to spend your time on, there is a very good chance you would be directionless and unhappy!

Have you ever wondered about successful people that commit suicide? There are many examples. These people didn't have to work, and were what many would consider rich (financially speaking), why were they so unhappy? The answer is that money or financial freedom was not the determining factor in their level of satisfaction in life. I would pick that they lacked purpose, a sense of fulfilment, and self-worth.

I would like to suggest that when going against your instincts and seeking out uncomfortable situations, you will get more out of your life. Think about anyone that has achieved anything great in life. If humans didn't seek out uncomfortable activities, we wouldn't have electricity, or indoor plumbing (way too much thinking involved), we wouldn't have travelled to other countries (not very comfortable on a boat into the unknown), we would probably have died out, being such a hopeless species! People that do things that are perceived as crazy by others, do so for the sense of satisfaction that doing something challenging provides. Running around the block isn't much of a challenge (for most people anyway), running the length of your home country is!

Someone quoted a statistic to me about the alarming rates of death once people retire from work. I also recall reading about studies (you got me, I said no studies, but this wasn't to do with food!) where retired professional men were asked to go away to a retreat and act as if it were twenty years ago (as if their careers were in full swing). Amazing changes in their health and sense of wellbeing were reported. I think that once retired, if people are not careful, they can lose much of the purpose and satisfaction that working for a living brings. We have been conditioned to think that we don't enjoy work ("thank god it's Friday"), but I think we would be much happier if we changed our way of viewing work from a drag, to something that is massively helping with our sense of purpose in life. I know, I know, some people's jobs are genuinely horrible, but I still think if you looked hard enough you could find a positive aspect to focus on, while you keep your eyes open for something else. You will get more of what you focus on, so if you focus on the negative aspects of your job, guess what you will get more of?

Back to you and your weight loss. I'm picking that losing weight is unlikely to be your purpose in life. It is more likely to be something you would like to have taken care of and then not need to think about again. To do this, you need to understand that seeking out discomfort is a good thing, not a bad thing! This applies to any number of areas of life and once you understand it, you will be able to observe it in others, or more likely you will be able to see how others avoid discomfort, which is keeping them from growing, and ultimately from being happy.

Imagine your mindset being to avoid discomfort at all costs. How do you think you would approach life? Let's use your work as an example. Here is a list of not uncommon actions of someone that avoids discomfort at work:

1. Comes in as late as possible.
2. Leaves as early as possible.
3. Would never miss a break no matter how busy, as "I am entitled to it".
4. Never helps overworked team members, thinking "that is not my problem".
5. Does as little as possible while on the job.
6. Doesn't provide input during meetings.
7. Not interested in learning new tasks or developing themselves. Only does additional training when forced to.

How happy do you think this person would be? What if they won the lottery and didn't have to go to work ever again? Do you think they would be happy? They may feel happy about not needing to go to work, but what would be their purpose in life? Would they use the money to enrich the lives of those around them? Would they donate generously to charities? I would guess that unless their attitude was majorly overhauled, their life would lack direction, and as they are not feeling any discomfort, how can they appreciate all the comfort they now have?

Have you ever done anything that was challenging for you? Perhaps you have completed a university or college degree? Perhaps you have run a marathon, written a book, or started a business. How did you feel when you were doing it? You probably had thoughts like "why am I doing this", or "how can I get out of this?". Believe me, I have had these thoughts while writing this book! The old me would have never finished it, but luckily, I changed some time ago to the kind of person that finishes things!

What about when you finished the challenging thing? Did you feel good about it? Did you feel proud of yourself? I sure hope you did, because that is where your happiness comes from. If you can do the things you say you will do, even when you don't feel like doing them, you will build amazing self-confidence, and through placing yourself into uncomfortable situations regularly, you will be able to more easily handle all the little challenges that life throws at you.

Anyway, I have digressed again. Back to weight loss. If you have the mindset that you should seek comfort, then you will likely fail. You have heard the term comfort food! That is a term for people that don't want to improve and want to remain stuck being over-weight and unhappy and worst of all, blaming everyone else for it! You are not that person. You are now the type that understands that discomfort is awesome because that is where the progress is!

Once this clicked for me, all aspects of life were easier. With this understanding of the need to be uncomfortable and seek out uncomfortable situations, I now do odd things like, get up really early, have a cold shower, and not eat breakfast. These simple actions give me the mental satisfaction of knowing that I am doing things each day that make me uncomfortable (though to be fair, I am very used to these now and don't really feel discomfort). While early morning rising and cold showers have nothing to do with what I eat, they are part of the mindset shift that allows me to enjoy situations that could be perceived as uncomfortable. For example, not wanting to eat the chocolate biscuits that are available for everyone at the work meeting, and wanting to eat a handful of almonds instead.

You may be thinking, "wait a minute, didn't you say that you look at bad food and see poison? Now you are saying that you seek discomfort. How can it be uncomfortable if you already see it as poison?" Excellent question. In order to truly not want to eat junk food or high sugar 'treats', you need to understand that seeking discomfort is a good thing. You will then be open to doing things that you previously would avoid, due to the feelings of deprivation or discomfort. Now that you no longer see discomfort as bad, you will soon take actions that you can be proud of and great things will happen, such as curing addiction to sugar and seeing the poison that it really is.

To put it more simply, you will see that what you previously thought was hard, is actually easy, and what you previously thought was easy, is actually hard. It is very easy to eat satisfying meals such as steak and salad, or my pancakes (see the recipe section of this book), and quality bacon (you know the kind from your local butcher, not full of water and preservatives!), while not having to worry about putting on weight or your health suffering. It is _not_ easy eating rubbish food, constantly feeling guilty and deprived, out of breath, lethargic, having low self-esteem, and blaming others for your troubles!

I really hope this is clear. It is critical to understand this concept, so please read it again if it doesn't sink in the first time. This should complete your understanding of the changes required to be a lean and healthy person. There should be no doubt in your mind that you are the type of person that doesn't _want_ to eat junk food for comfort. You don't seek comfort food, because you know that seeking comfort is not the answer, and your progress in life is made by seeking out uncomfortable situations. You know that by accepting that discomfort is awesome, you have already won your battle with food, and that you will have no feelings of deprivation or desire to eat bad food. Congratulations!

Part 3- Putting This All Together in the Real World

So now, you have changed and are eating well. You have made the mental shift required to never again see pizza (excluding my special pizza of course), sugary drinks, vegetable oils, doughnuts, empty carbs, etc. as a treat that you must resist using will power. Instead, you now see this sort of food as poison. Why would I ingest this poison? Is what you might say to yourself. We need to make sure that you can function in the real world, with temptations and other influences everywhere.

Be Prepared with a Game Plan in Your Head

You are going to need to be ready for potentially awkward moments (away from the safety of your own kitchen) where you are required to politely turn down food, possibly offending the clueless, but well-meaning preparer of the nasty 'treats' that have previously ruined your waistline.

What do you say to this person? Will they be offended? What if you are out for dinner and there is only processed rubbish on the menu? Do you go hungry? Do you eat it "just this once"? You may find this annoying, but I can't answer this for you. You need to figure out what you are prepared to accept in your diet. Can you ensure that not one gram of sugar or vegetable oil or processed food passes your lips? Well, you can try, but good luck with that! Any sort of meal that has been prepared by someone other than you, has the potential to include some nasty stuff.

Personally, I refuse to eat sugary food wherever possible. If I am in a situation where I am offered it, I will usually say something like "that looks amazing (for poison), but not for me thanks". No need to make a big deal. Definitely not the time to announce that everyone else in the room is on a fast track to type 2 diabetes!

At the office, we regularly have shared meals. You know, a 'potluck' lunch. Anyway, my colleagues are well and truly used to me and know that I will not touch any of the bad stuff. I just bring along something that I do want to eat.

If I eat chocolate, it is the darkest kind (like 95% cocoa), and if I want a sweet treat, I will go for something like low carb biscuits and whipped cream, or find a recipe online for whatever I fancy. You can find some pretty amazing cheesecake options that have a base made from cashews or almonds and are topped with coconut cream!

The point is that it is entirely possible to set yourself some standards in advance so as you know what you are willing or unwilling to accept.

What About Cheat Days?

If you go six days being 'good', then surely one day of 'cheating' won't hurt, right? Well, maybe. The problem I see with cheat days is not dissimilar for the smoker that tries to "only smoke socially", or "only on weekends". Again, that mindset change has not occurred. If you see the rubbish food as poison, you genuinely do not want to eat it. That is one of the most critical parts of this book. To me, if you filled a table with chocolates, cakes, sweets, and pies, I genuinely would not want to eat it. The reason- I changed!

If you were to use regular cheat days, there is every chance that you could end up holding out until you make it to your cheat day and you can finally go crazy. To me, that is a sure-fire way to end up feeling deprived, and therefore, reliant on that not so good friend, will power.

Don't Feel Deprived, Feel Sorry for Them

We have touched on this earlier, but I think it is worth revisiting. You will very likely encounter people, who, once they see the change in you, will attempt to ridicule you, or make you feel silly for going against the crowd. They are scared, and deep down know that they are not doing what they should to look after themselves. Their attempts to bring you down are nothing more than a manifestation of their fear. You should not feel deprived, bad, or silly. The nasty side of humans is to try to bring those that succeed back to the level of the majority. You should feel sorry for them!

One thing that will go through your mind is, "I have friends and family that love to scoff down doughnuts and pies, I bet I can share what I have read in this book and help them lose weight". With your newfound confidence and understanding of the psychology of eating, you may be tempted to reach out to these people, with the best of intentions. Caution! Tread carefully here! It is entirely possible, that despite your honourable intentions, to someone that is not ready to change, your help may be seen as interfering, and "ramming it down my throat". You are best to wait until they have decided to improve themselves. Perhaps they will if they pick up this book.

What will make an impact on your family and friends is seeing the change in you. When you show up looking awesome, bursting with energy, and loving life, they won't help but want to know about your success. Actually, this can be a good way to see what your friends are really like. The good ones will be genuinely happy for you and encouraging. There may be some that say things (behind your back, of course) like "I don't think it will last", or "that can't be healthy". They will be the ones that try to make fun of you if you turn down the sugary dessert at a dinner party, or when you look for a healthy alternative to a burger when you are on a road trip. You might want to reconsider if you want these people in your life!

If you want to stay in the world of a lean and happy person, you don't need the negativity of such people. Negative people suck the life out of you, and compromise the change you have made in yourself. You may think that you can change these people if you can just get across to them how much better life is when you are being pulled towards a lean and happy life. The great motivator, Les Brown (look him up on YouTube if you want to feel inspired), says that you shouldn't try to change those around you, because it's a full-time job just changing yourself! Don't take the focus away from changing yourself.

How to Deal with the Bad Food That Is Everywhere

I won't kid you; this part is tricky. You will find yourself in situations where the food choices are pretty crappy. Just the other day, I was at a conference where I knew that lunch was being provided. Against my better judgement, I thought that there might be enough healthy options available that I wouldn't need to pack my own lunch and be "that person". You know, the one that pulls out a cooler bag with their own special lunch, not wanting to eat what the commoners are having.

Well, this was a good reminder for me. I should have been "that person", as I really don't care these days if I am the only one eating a healthy lunch. By the way, if you have read through this book, you will know that by healthy, I don't just mean a salad or carrot sticks. That packed lunch could be leftover roast pork! What I didn't want to eat was the 'healthy' option from the lunch provided. It was one of those deals where lunch arrives in boxes with different ones to choose from. The 'healthy' one included a sandwich made from white bread and a cookie made from white flour. Not what I want to be eating!

The reason I am sharing this fascinating lunchtime story is that, even after knowing what I need to do and not even wanting the stupid lunch that gets fed to the masses, I still slip up sometimes. That is okay, it happens. What would not be okay is to tell myself that I can't control what I eat. Next time, I will make sure I pack my own lunch in a cooler bag. Simple. I don't care if that makes me "weird". I would much rather be weird than wander around like the rest of the world on a fast track to poor health!

Final Thoughts

We are at the end of the line now. I have shared everything that I need to share. Let's quickly summarise the key messages to take out of this book:

1. For things to change, you have to change - you can change, and by getting this far, you will have changed. This means that you are the one that is in control, not the outside world. Change is as simple as deciding to.

2. Become a lean and healthy person – when you make the mental shift that you are no longer an overweight person, the physical

one will inevitably follow. Healthy people don't want to eat empty carbs and sugary crap all the time.

3. You don't need will power or any of the stories you tell yourself. Once you have changed your mindset, it becomes easy to turn away junk food, because you don't want it anymore!

4. You can definitely enjoy food without 'giving up' the foods you love. Change your mindset, and the foods you love will change!

5. By changing who you are, there is no need for that feeling of "this is going well but won't last" that traditional calorie counting or restrictive dieting brings.

6. Remember to stop seeking comfort!

Final, Final Thoughts!

Okay, so in this book, I have shared my story and what I have learned along the way. Again, mine is not a story of someone that was super big and told by their doctor, friends, and family that they needed to lose weight to save their life. Maybe that was you? Maybe you are someone that has searched online for ways to lose weight and came across this book. I was never a big believer in fate or the universe and other such hippie nonsense (though as I get older, I'm becoming more open to it). However, for some reason, this book has found its way into your life. Maybe it was meant to be. Maybe you put sufficient positive energy into the world that the universe decided to send this book your way. Okay, I still don't know if I believe that sort of mumbo jumbo just yet, but I do hope that this book has helped you change the person that you are, into a lean and healthy one. Happy eating!